A Glint of Light

poems by

Fredric Hildebrand

Finishing Line Press
Georgetown, Kentucky

A Glint of Light

Copyright © 2020 by Fredric Hildebrand
ISBN 978-1-64662-383-9 First Edition
All rights reserved under International and Pan-American Copyright Conventions. No part of this book may be reproduced in any manner whatsoever without written permission from the publisher, except in the case of brief quotations embodied in critical articles and reviews.

ACKNOWLEDGMENTS

My thanks to the editors of the following publications where some of the poems in this collection first appeared, sometimes in slightly different versions:

Amethyst Review ~ "October Morning"
ArtAscent ~ "The Forest Trail"
Bramble ~ "Charm for Sleep"
The Raven Review ~ "A Funeral;" "Autumn Frost"
Right-Hand Pointing ~ "The Sound of Spring"
Verse-Virtual ~ "At the Ojibwa All-Night Diner;" "On the Way to the Mayo Clinic;" "Psalm;" The Night Train"

Publisher: Leah Huete de Maines
Editor: Christen Kincaid
Cover Art: Kathryn A. Wedge, KathrynWedge.com
Author Photo: Frederic Hildebrand
Cover Design: Elizabeth Maines McCleavy

Order online: www.finishinglinepress.com
              also available on amazon.com

Author inquiries and mail orders:
Finishing Line Press
P. O. Box 1626
Georgetown, Kentucky 40324
U. S. A.

Table of Contents

At the Ojibwa All-Night Diner 1

On the Way to the Mayo Clinic 2

Today the Tree Fell 4

September 1, 8 a.m. 5

October Morning 6

In a Hospital: 3 a.m. 7

A Funeral 8

November Evening 9

Autumn Frost 10

Psalm 11

At a Bend in the Road 12

Spring Equinox 13

How Many Mornings 14

The Sound of Spring 15

At the Polling Place 16

The Hatchet 18

Spring Moment 19

Geese in April 20

Gate F2, O'Hare Airport 21

Above the Flambeau River 22

Prairie Morning 23

Charm For Sleep 25

Woodsmoke Days 26

The Night Train 27

The Forest Trail 28

At the Ojibwa All-Night Diner

Nothing else open this time of night
between Spooner and Woodruff. Old man
and woman shuffle to the first table. Worn
wood chairs scrape across the chipped

linoleum floor as they sit. Waitress
scribbles on her green pad, jet black eyes
and hair, and teenage resignation. Fry cook
father slumps in his chair and reads

a newspaper. Kitchen bell interrupts Hank
Williams belting *"I'm So Lonesome I
Could Cry"* on the chrome and neon Wurlitzer.
Old man steadies his sandwich, probably

a cold ham and cheese on whole wheat
with mustard and onion but no pickle,
carefully cuts it corner to corner, silently
slides one half onto his wife's plate as she

wearily adjusts her glasses and unrolls
a napkin. Hank's voice wails: *"Did you ever
see a night so slow as time goes draggin' by?
I'm so lonesome I could cry."*

On the Way to the Mayo Clinic

Coffee tastes the same
as so many years ago,
black and burned.
The same diner,
probably the same booth.

"You're doing fine,"
the doctor had said,
but you weren't, not
with scars, one breast,
a limp, and memory loss.

But at that moment
you were past caring
about doctors and battles
with disease. You didn't eat,
frustrated by your tremor

and too proud to be fed.
Three times was enough, you said,
smiling, and maybe we wouldn't
make the trip again. You didn't
want to fight anymore.

Within weeks the cancer returned
a fourth time, quicker and more
relentless than before, pushing
your chest outwards, wrapping
around your organs, and leaving
you breathless and drained.

Yet you said nothing and endured it.
Then swallowing became impossible
and you finally had enough. Still smiling,
with your dignity intact, you slipped away
peacefully.

Now with pain and admiration
I look for your courage
in this coffee cup.

Today the Tree Fell

It died of old age,
like a man, its body
ravaged at the last.

We had measured time
by it, reached our arms
around to touch finger

tips. Our feelings were
its yearly rings. Now
our fears, age, time.

The tree held life.
Birds and squirrels
made memories in its

branches. Raccoons,
owls in its cavities
until the day it fell.

Death a dull thud.
Arms to catch the fall
long gone. Now the body

exposed, a gut of grubs
and hollowness,
descending into grass.

September 1, 8 a.m.

Dawn is late.
The somber darkness
hangs on.

Hidden sounds carry
through the mist;
a loon's fluttering call,

the *kik, kik, kik*
of an eagle.
Slowly the fog yields

to the crisp and urgent morning.
Still there is no seeing
the lake, only reflected images:

the black and green forest,
the gray and heavy sky,
on a still surface.

How glorious, cloaked
in this whisper moment,
everything beautiful around me.

October Morning

The maple
this morning

shadow tree
ghost tree

black leaves haunt
the night sky

the gray grass
gloomy yard

embers wait
dawn to soak

this day in color
my rising light.

In a Hospital: 3 a.m.

A body outstretched on a table.
Tubes, catheters, blood.

The circle of gloves and gowns
around him widens slowly.

Alarms and machines unhooked
and turned off one by one.

Found in the street, his young
vanquished heart, shocked but

never awake.
In silence the kinship of our

survival. Prayers for husbands,
fathers, sons, brothers.

The chaplain says he has no family.
We lift his death onto a cart,

cloak him in a snow-white sheet,
wheel him through the doors

which open and close on their own.

A Funeral

In the twilight a church bell
tolls for the neighbor's son.

Nearby a weathered shed,
a broken farmer unable
to speak of grief.

Woodsmoke, heat, glowing coals.
Hammer and tongs, and despair.

Plowshares must be repaired before spring,
a father's anguish in each blow.

The hammer and steel ring.

November Evening

Bitter dusk descends.
Wet leaves carpet the grimy ground.
The chill pines shiver.

Owl's screech darkens the night.

Blackness under the surface.

Then the stars, pinprick white.
A curve of light atones for
the grim day.

Owl flies away.

Autumn Frost

Dogs wait patiently at the door.
Outside the frozen leaves.
Over the twilight roof,
moon like white muslin.
Orion rises in the southern sky.

My father said, "We're waiting for winter now."
His death was another season, long.
That evening the cold, woodsmoke waiting.

Silence now except a faint whispering.
Then great flakes of wet snow.
I turn to the sky; I receive the blessing.
Dogs wait patiently at the door.

Psalm

I lift mine eyes unto the hills,
from whence cometh the tree that
gave of the wood for this fire,
and the gift of this pitch-crackling,
dog-snoring, soul-warming, winter
moment of peace.

Lord, Master of beauty and this moment,
thank you for bringing me here.
You have come to my rescue again and again.
You know my comings and goings.
May I be eternally grateful.

Amen.

At a Bend in the Road

At a bend in the road
a fallen fence, chained
gate, faded farmhouse.

Empty corncribs shudder
together before the north wind.

Near the once-red barn
and rusted pickup, no tracks.

An old farmer splits wood
on a battered stump, his

frayed flannel, blood
against the covering snow.

Maybe in spring there will be flowers.

Spring Equinox

Nothing but white,
the ground, the light.

The day waits for spring.
Everything is waiting:

the wheelbarrow
against the maple,

the maple itself.
The upturned bucket.

Even the slinking
fog and gray clouds

would sooner be gone.
A robin on the wire

between my house
and the corner pole

wants to sing.

How Many Mornings

How many mornings have I been
unimpressed by the dawn,
taking no notice of another day.

But somehow today I am
awake to the joy in all:
in the creaking floor of this divine,
drafty old house,
in the faithful, angelic tail wag,
in the daily chapel of yogurt and berries,
in the holy nuthatches at the window feeder,

in the glorious crunching of cold snow
underfoot as when at age seven
I winter-walked with my father,
holding his hand.

There is God in all these things,
Praise them.

The Sound of Spring

I recall a blackbird
perched on our chimney,

and the melting snow,
and the ice gone overnight,
and the homecoming

of mallards, mergansers,
goldeneyes, and geese
to the open river,

and the end of the slowed
season with neighbors
now out of their houses,

this blackbird

warming herself and singing
to a mate in the treetops
and down the chimney to me,

not exactly the bird
but the cleansing
rains and green maple
days that followed her.

At the Polling Place

In the early spring
wind the flag snaps
and tugs at the pole
beside the door

of the old boathouse,
repurposed for our
civic duty. Mid-day
voters form a line

to enter. Suits, uniforms,
walkers. Murmurs
of a late spring snow.
A dog sleeps inside

the door. Name and
address triple checked
at a table decorated
with red, white, and blue.

Gray-haired volunteers
remember my parents.
I darken the circles
for a slate of candidates

and approve the school
referendum. At the exit,
handshakes, a percolator
of coffee, a stack of cups,

a sign reading,
"Poll Workers Only."
Inducements for voters
are not permitted,

I am told. Outside
the flag pulley clinks
on the pole. Across
the river the red

brick faces of the
library and town hall.
Beyond stretches the
Republic I love.

The Hatchet

Rust-caked
handle missing
right-handed

hewing bevel
long forgotten
waiting to work

its singular purpose
and shaming our
disconnected lives

new hickory handle
sleek steel head
restored for duty

no beams to carve
but the kindling box
needs filling

Even in mundane work
a sharpened edge
makes a proud bite.

Spring Moment

Gloves, a rake,
the winter worn yard.

A blackbird
warns me off.

I stand my ground.
He sticks to his branch.

Satisfied we were
both wasting our time

he flies off, leaving
a vision of brilliant

red and yellow
on a black wing

and a moment
that should last

forever but slides

by like water.

Geese in April

The sky is gray
and low. An old

man in a black
overcoat walks

a yellow dog.
Above, a flock

of geese honks.
The dog lifts its

face to the sky.
The man looks up

too. "Geese," says
the man to the dog,

"geese," and he
laughs.

The dog looks
at him and wags

its tail. The man
smiles.

Two friends, faces
turned to the sky

as if to receive
this blessing.

Gate F2, O'Hare Airport

We do not choose our company.
Among my fellow travelers

all recognition is suspended.
Electronic devices, earpieces,

expressions of private absorption
to fend off comment.

Sitting together we say nothing.
We must have something to share:

the relief of leaving,
the anticipation of arrival,

or the hope for something more - -
possibly a conversation

with someone, face to face.

Above the Flambeau River

High on a ridge,
a path leads
to a small
grass meadow

edged with aspen
and white pine.
The sun high,
the air cool.

Near a cluster
of coneflowers
a glint of light.
On hands and knees

parting sedge grass,
an arrowhead,
speckled white,
flaked and sharp

from careful tooling.
They came to camp
here. This meadow.
This north woods

of ancient hunters.
I follow their
trail.

Prairie Morning

On the far side
of the grassland
light filters
through aspens
like water
rushing
into an empty
riverbed.

A warbler
chirps.
A white-tailed
deer
pauses
mid-trail
before vanishing
in the switchgrass.

Wolf tracks
fresh from
the night.
The shadow
of an osprey
chased
by
the osprey.

At the crest
of a low hill,
the wide
landscape.
Wildflowers
paint the prairie
under a sapphire
sky.

A burbling
bobolink
picks up
the rustling
breeze
and joins it
to a flood
of song.

Charm for Sleep

Ready the downy cradle.
Pull tight the bedclothes.
Open wide the window.
Let in the night spirits.

But slumber does not come.
Worry spins me awake.
Hypnos, Morpheus, Masters
of Night; strike me with your sleep!

Borne from this midnight moment,
into the deepening winter
blackness, into the house
of the gods, I am born

into the red fox setting stealthy prints in the silver snow
into the basswood bending against the biting wind
into the nightjar dancing unseen in the darkness
into the moon radiating its wisp of white

Floating upward on the altar
of the gods the heavens surround me.
Into their spell I leap,
at peace and once more asleep.

Woodsmoke Days

These are the days we dreamed
of, woodsmoke drifting over
cabin roof, dogs snoring
at our feet. Our children

as safe as they'll ever be,
making their way in far off
cities. Our debts are paid.

All day we laugh and hold
hands, counting years we don't
believe have passed and years
of mystery ahead.

At night we lie touching for hours,
then the quiet woods and the owls
so close.

This is our life.

This is our love.

The Night Train

Sometimes when I lie awake
and hear the piercing whistle,
the night seems blacker,

the desolation of sorrow
greater. I think of loneliness
and the vast coldness that can

separate people. These thoughts
spin like a child pedaling
a tricycle in endless

circles. Then the train rumbles
away and the deep silence
returns. I hear her breathing,

its peaceful, calming rhythm.
The space of melancholy grows
smaller and the spinning stops.

I think of the train reaching
the next town, I embrace love and hope,
and remember how fortunate I am.

The Forest Trail

The old rail bed underfoot
has softened only slightly
from the recent rain that
has dampened my spirit.

Late in the afternoon
the slanting light of
the fall day is fading
and the gray horizon

unrolls from the east.
The crisp air signals
the coming change
from harvest to sleep.

Distantly the drone
of a tractor threads
the silence; it passes
and is gone.

The trees beside the path
glow red and gold.
It is this quiet I love.
In the moment a sudden

breeze showers me
in a heaven of falling colors,
like a baptism of cleansing rain.
I can begin again.

Fredric Hildebrand began writing poetry after retiring from medical practice in 2017. His poems have been published in numerous journals, including *Amethyst Review*, *Red-Eft Review*, and *Right Hand Pointing*. Recent work has appeared in *The MacGuffin* and *Third Wednesday*. He is the author of the chapbook *Northern Portrait* (Kelsay Books, 2020), and he received honorable mention awards from the Mill Prize for Poetry in 2018 and 2019.

www.ingramcontent.com/pod-product-compliance
Lightning Source LLC
LaVergne TN
LVHW041514070426
835507LV00012B/1575